This book is dedicated to the memory of my mother

Lennie Corey (nee Newell)

25/7/1943 - 26/6/2007

Acknowledgements

There are many people whom I have to thank for various reasons.
Firstly I have to acknowledge the late Dr. Ann Hamlin, who wrote most of the image captions for this book. She gave freely of her knowledge and time, and was always enthusiastic and encouraging at every stage of her involvement: for this I will always be grateful.
Victor Sloan not only wrote the introduction, but was my tutor and mentor during the early part of my career. He remains always ready and willing to help in whatever way is necessary.
My colleagues in the NIEA, who have been there for support and inspiration, especially James and Gail who always know the right thing to say and when, without ever trying to do so.
My wife Amanda and our children Nathaniel and Charlotte for always being there with a smile and a hug, and the intellect and logic only a child can bring.
And lastly to my family for their unquestioning support over many, many years.

Tony.

Introduction

Tony Corey's highly atmospheric photographic images are a result of a marriage between traditional – film and darkroom chemical processes – and digital photographic techniques. He captures these compositions using black and white infrared film in his analogue camera, then develops the film and prints the images onto silver gelatine photographic paper.

The magical quality of these pictures are then further enhanced by employing traditional photographic techniques, including sepia toning, before applying dyes, toners or paints to selective areas by hand and with great subtlety, to the resulting photographic print surfaces. The images are then scanned before final adjustments are made, and then printed onto digital photographic paper.

The infrared film captures the sun's reflected infrared radiation, causing strange effects, such as leaves and green foliage recording as white or light grey. Tony's use of infrared produces spectacular darkened skies, and this, contrasted against the white foliage and white clouds, along with his strong composition, produces dramatic and ghostly imagery.

The pictures are mythical and literary, calling to mind the spirit of Irish poetry. They are timeless, and concern the spirit of place, creating the feeling of an historic image. It is almost as if Tony was the first person ever to visit these places - there is no evidence of contemporary human interference. In preserving these places and their beauty for future generations, he evokes imagery from photography's beginnings.

Tony has been producing his superb fine art imagery for twenty five years. His works have been exhibited throughout the world. He is also represented in numerous private and public collections. He was one of the artists selected by Lucy Lippard, the renowned New York based art critic and writer of the definitive book on Pop Art, to represent Ireland in a prestigious exhibition which toured USA, Canada and Europe.

Victor Sloan MBE RUA FRPS

Tirnony Dolmen, Co. Londonderry

This single chamber tomb lies at the verge of a by-road. The chamber was substantially intact with a large capstone supported by two portal stones over 1m high with 5 other stones forming the back and sides.
1.7km north-west of Maghera.

Glenknock or Cloghogle, Co. Tyrone

Standing on flat ground, this megalithic tomb is orientated north-south. The megalith is disturbed but it is possible to identify a broken capstone, a jamb, several side stones and traces of a cairn. These are probably the remains of a portal tomb or 'dolmen', a type of burial monument dating from the late Neolithic period. This was usually a single burial chamber, roofed with a large capstone supported by two tall uprights (the portals) and sloped down to a single back-stone.
This tomb is 2.5km north-north-east of Newtownstewart.

Legananny Dolmen, Co. Down

This well-known portal tomb stands on the south side of Slieve Croob and has magnificent views south to the Mourne Mountains. The large coffin-like capstone is neatly balanced on three unusually tall supports, a maximum of 1.8m high. There are slight remains of a cairn around the monument and an early record shows that urns were found in the dolmen.
8km north-west of Castlewellan, off the main Castlewellan to Banbridge Road.

Rough Fort, Co. Down

This Early Christian rath (defended farmstead) is on high ground with housing developments all around. It is well preserved and the high central area is surrounded by a deep ditch, a bank and an outer ditch missing on the south-east, where it is covered by the Moira to Kilmore Road. A causeway on the east gave access to the central area. The site has not been excavated, but it probably contained several circular wooden or wickerwork farmers' houses, dating from the 8th or 9th century AD.
The site is 0.5km west of Moira.

Ballynoe Stone Circle, Co. Down

This complex prehistoric monument is the result of long development in the Late Neolithic and Early Bronze Age. The site now appears as a large circle, 33m in diameter, of closely-spaced upright stones surrounding an oval mound. There are some outlying monoliths (single standing stones). Excavations in 1937-8 revealed a rectangular stone cist (box-like structure) at each end of the mound, containing cremated bones. The earthen mound covered a low cairn of stones.
4km south of Downpatrick.

Berrysfort Standing Stone, Co. Tyrone

This site on the outskirts of Castlederg stands on a low hill on the south bank of the River Derg, with good views of the immediate vicinity and to higher ground in the distance. The pillar stands an impressive 2.3m tall and is sub-rectangular in cross section, tapering to its rounded tip. It may mark a prehistoric grave, routeway or boundary.
1.1km south-east of Castlederg.

Boa Island Figure, Co. Fermanagh

This stone figure of 'Janus' type stands in Caldragh graveyard, Dreenan townland at the west end of Boa Island (near the main road from Pettigo to Belleek which crosses the island). The graveyard, still in use, is incorporated in an early ecclesiastical enclosure. The twin cross-armed figures of the idol stand back to back. The effigy is very unusual; some features such as the long pointed faces, suggest a prehistoric date while others have argued for an Early Christian origin. Another carved effigy brought to Caldragh from Lusty More Island for safety has been erected nearby.
10km west of Kesh on the Belleek Road.

Kilnasaggart Pillar Stone, Co. Armagh

This tall, inscribed granite pillar stone (2.18m) stands on the ancient route known as the Slighe Miodluachra where it runs through the Moyry Pass. It is situated in an ancient circular graveyard some 50m in diameter. The inscription, 'IN LOC SO TANIMMARNI Ternohc Mac Ceran Bic er cul Peter Apstel' tells of the dedication of the area by Ternoc, son of Ceran Bic, under the patronage of Peter the Apostle. Ternoc's death is recorded in the annals at AD 714 or 716. This is, therefore, the oldest datable inscription in Ireland and was erected around AD 700. There are three crosses carved on the south-east face and ten on the north-west.
2km south of Jonesborough in Edenappa townland.

Navan Fort, Co. Armagh

This large circular-plan earthwork enclosure has been identified as the historic Emhain Macha, chief 'residence' of the kings of Ulster and prominent as the capital of the province in heroic literature and legend. The monument surrounds a grassy drumlin and is some 12 acres in extent. The enclosing bank is outside and downslope from the ditch. This, coupled with the evidence from excavations which have taken place since the 1960s, shows that the monument was an Iron Age sanctuary or religious site, that was built in the early first century BC. With sites like Tara, Co. Meath and Cruachan, Co. Roscommon, Dun Ailne in Co. Kildare and the Rock of Cashel Co. Tipperary, Navan is identified as one of the ancient provincial 'royal' sites of Ireland.

The summit of the hill, enclosed by the earthwork, is occupied by a large mound, 60m in diameter and 5m high, built at the same time as the enclosure. It may have been used for the inauguration of prehistoric rulers and as a focus for community festivals. Navan Fort is the latest monument in a landscape with remains dating from the Neolithic period and the Bronze Age.

3.2km west of Armagh, off the road to Killylea.

Ardboe Cross, Co. Tyrone

On a rocky height, overlooking Lough Neagh, the finest cross in the north marks the site of an Early Christan church, perhaps a monastery. Though weathered and battered, especially the head, the cross has a rich scheme of figurative decoration. This is the east side with old testament scenes : Adam and Eve at the base, then the Sacrifice of Isaac, Daniel in the Lions' Den and the Children in the Fiery Furnace. There is a judgement scene on the head, with scales underneath for the weighing of souls. The fence was put up in the 1930s because local people were taking chips off the cross to bring good fortune in America.
8km east-south-east of Coagh.

Nendrum Monastery, Co. Down

Nendrum, an island site in Strangford Lough, is the best example in Northern Ireland of an early monastery. It has three concentric stone enclosures, the substantial remains of a church, a round tower, workshops and other features. This view of the inner enclosure shows the church (west wall and west door partly reconstructed in the 1920s) and the stump of the round tower, both perhaps from the 10th century. The church was associated with St. Mochaoi, a Benedictine foundation followed in the late 12th century, and a parish church was here until it was abandoned for the mainland in the 15th century. 10km south-east of Comber, on Mahee Island, off the Comber - Downpatrick road.

Donaghmore Cross, Co. Tyrone

This cross was re-erected at the road junction at the west end of the village street, outside the old graveyard. It is made up of parts of two different crosses, similar but with rather different edge mouldings. This is the east face with New Testament scenes, from the Annunciation to the Shepherds at the base to the Crucifixion on the head. It probably dates from the 10th century. The graveyard trees are visible behind the cross.
At the top of Main Street, in the centre of Donaghmore town.

Devenish Island, Co Fermanagh

This is the most significant of the numerous island monasteries of Lough Erne. The site was founded in the 6th century by Saint Molaise. It was raided by Vikings in 837. In the Middle Ages it became St Mary's Augustinian Priory and was used as a parish church. A 12th-century church and a round tower testify to the prestige of the site at the end of the Early Christian period, and the ruins of the15th-century Abbey church and cloister correspond to the site's history. There is also an enclosure and other earthworks of uncertain date and the site of a holy well.
An island on Lough Erne, 2.4km downstream from Enniskillen

Kilbroney, Co. Down

This 2.3m high, unringed cross stands in the graveyard around the ruins of a medieval church built on an earlier monastic site. There are beautiful views to the Mournes. The cross has a regular outline with three-quarter-round sunken hollows at the angles of shaft and arms. Both main faces of the cross are covered in geometric ornament, now weathered. An Early Christian bronze bell from Kilbroney (now in Rostrevor RC church) has been associated with St. Bronach, patroness of the site (Bronach's Church). The ruined church dates from the 15th or 16th century and is 13m long. In the graveyard is another cross, 1m high, the upper part of which is shaped like a human figure with stumpy outstretched arms.
Kilbroney is 1km north of Rostrevor at the side of the Rostrevor - Hilltown road.

Dundrum Castle, Co. Down

Built on the site of an Early Christian period stronghold, Dunnadroma, the polygonal upper ward was begun in the 1180s or 1190s by John de Courcy. The circular keep, its upper parts re-modelled in the 15th century, was added shortly after 1200. In 1210 the castle was captured by King John and it passed to the Earls of Ulster in 1227. The twin-towered gatehouse was probably added in the 1260s and the outer ward was extended down the hillside some time after that. The castle was in ruins by 1333, but in the later middle ages it was a stronghold of the Magennises. In 1636 Dundrum Castle was granted to Sir Francis Blundell who erected an L-shaped house, now a gaunt ruin in the lower ward.
The site is high on a hill outside Dundrum village overlooking Dundrum Bay and the main Newcastle-Belfast Road.

Grey Abbey, Co. Down

The abbey ruins stand in beautiful grounds at the east edge of Greyabbey village, adjoining the Rosemount estate. This Cistercian abbey was founded in 1193 by John de Courcy's wife Affreca. East of the abbey church is the parish graveyard, perhaps on the site of the monks' cemetery. This view shows the east end of the church from the graveyard with two tiers of narrow pointed lancet windows. Grey Abbey has been described as the first truly Gothic church in Ireland, dating from the early 13th century.
On Church Street, Grey Abbey.

Carrickfergus Castle, Co. Antrim

The original structure, the great keep at the seaward end of the rock promontory, was built in the 1180s by John De Courcy, who conquered parts of east Ulster. The middle ward was added around 1220 with a postern gate to the sea. The outer ward and gatehouse facing the town at the landward end of the promontry were probably built in the 1230s. Later the castle was altered during its long history as a military stronghold, for defence using firearms and artillery. The castle was besieged by King John in 1210 and by Edward Bruce in 1315. It was captured briefly by the French under General Thurot in 1760. It remained garrisoned until 1928 and was used as an air-raid shelter in World War II. The castle is the most impressive military fortification in Ulster and is open to the public with displays about its architectural development, its place in history and the influence of the Normans.
On the north shore of Belfast Lough, 15 km north-east of Belfast.

Inch Abbey, Co. Down

These beautiful ruins are set beside the River Quoile. They are the remains of a Cistercian abbey, founded by John De Courcy in about 1180, on the site of an earlier church. This view shows the church from the west, with the prominent grouped narrow windows at the east end. The holes visible in the masonry are 'putlog holes', which originally held wooden scaffolding poles. The site is enclosed by an earthwork and perfectly illustrates the solitude and tranquility sought by the Cistercians.
1.5km north-west of Downpatrick, reached by turning off the main Belfast road.

Harry Avery's Castle, Co. Tyrone

This castle stands on a prominent hill commanding important river valley routes. Named after Henry Aimhreidh O'Neill who died in 1392, it is an unusual and interesting ruin, a stone-built castle deep in Gaelic Ulster.
An artificially scarped natural mound formed an elevated bailey surrounded by a polygonal curtain wall with at least two projecting towers, all of which are now ruined to a low level.
At the south-west end is a tower that looks like a gate house, defended by a bridge-pit and entered between high D-shaped towers.
Located 1.2km south-west of Newtownstewart in Upper Deerpark townland and accessed by minor roads.

Dunluce Castle, Co. Antrim

Dramatically sited on a high, sea-tunneled rocky promontory. The castle probably occupies the site of an earlier fort, the presence of which is attested by a rock-cut souterrain of the Early Christian period. It is sometimes assumed that the castle was first built in the 14th or 15th century, but it is not documented until the 16th century and none of the visible masonry need be earlier. In the early 16th century, Dunluce was occupied by the MacQuillans, but they were ousted by Sorley Boy MacDonnell. The Castle was damaged during a siege with artillery in 1584, but was repaired and extended to become the chief seat of the MacDonnells. The Scottish-style gatehouse overlooking the bridge from the mainland is probably early 17th century in date. On the promontory behind it are remains of successive large houses and ancillary ranges protected by a curtain wall at the cliff edge and projecting towers. Remains of a rare Italianate loggia or covered way, lie near the inside of the south curtain wall. The rectangular mainland court has remains of 17th-century domestic and service buildings with visitor facilities.
5.5km east of Portrush.

Maghera Old Church, Co. Londonderry

St. Lurach founded his church on this site in the 6th century.
It was plundered by the Vikings in 1135 and burned. In the middle of the 12th century it was rebuilt and the uniquely decorated west door with its carved lintel is from this period. It was the seat of a Bishop until 1254, at which time it became the parish church of the area; a belfry was added in the 17th century with the church remaining in use until 1819.
Traditionally a cross-carved pillar stone in the graveyard is said to mark the burial place of St. Lurach.
In Maghera town, reached by turning off Main Street and Bank Square.

Kilclief, Co. Down

Standing on the shoreline overlooking the entrance to Strangford Lough, this tower-house with its square turrets overlooks the sea. Its construction is attributed to John Sely, Bishop of Down between 1413 and 1441, making it the oldest dated tower of this type in Co. Down. Sely was deprived of the Bishopric in 1441 after complaints of his living '*in castro de Kylcleth*' with a married woman. The castle is four-storeys high, the turrets on the east side facing the sea are united by a semi-circular arch forming a roof-level machicolation (a short stretch of battlement from which people at the door could be attacked). A 13th-century coffin lid is used as a lintel above the second-floor fireplace.

On the Strangford to Ardglass Road, 4km south of Strangford.

Derryloren Church, Co. Tyrone

The ruin stands in a graveyard beside the Ballinderry River, high above a bridge, on the SW edge of Cookstown. This substantial church occupies a site associated with an early saint called Luran, and later a medieval parish church. The present ruin is of a church built by the Planter, Alan Cook, at least partly on the foundations of the 13th-century church. The east window has distinctive tracery, characteristic of the 17th century. The church was lengthened in the 18th century at the west end, the sellcote and porch date from then. The church continued in use until 1822, though the graveyard is still in use.
0.8km from Cookstown town centre on the road to Omagh.

Drumnachose Old Church, Co. Londonderry

This was the medieval parish church of the Limavady area, on the site of an earlier church associated with St. Cainnech (Canice). There are substantial remains of a large, probably 13th century, church in a graveyard on a high mound above the main road, with trees all around. Here the view is to the east gable with its tall, narrow window, and the door in the north wall is visible on the left. Other interesting features include a cupboard in the south wall, a sloping plinth on the exterior east wall, and a cross carved near the east end of the north wall.

St. Cainnech is mainly associated with Kilkenny, but his family were from the Roe Valley area and during the middle ages this was the most important of a group of churches around the Roe. The church was reported to be ruined in 1622 and was replaced by a new church in Limavady.

2.5km east of Limavady, near Drummard Bridge.

Bovevagh Church, Co. Londonderry

This shows the approach to the south door of the old church at Bovevagh. The present church dates from the late medieval period but is on the site of an early church. A wooden church stood here in 1100, and the present ruin must be the last in a series of several churches on the site. West of the church is a distinctive saint's tomb with a cavity for the body and a hole for access to the remains, perhaps dating from the 12th century.
5km north-north-west of Dungiven.

Loughinisland Churches, Co. Down

Three churches in a large graveyard stand on an island reached by a causeway. The three churches probably date from the 13th to the early 17th centuries. This view shows the west gable of the biggest, probably 15th century church. Also visible is a burial vault and some of the numerous gravestones. This is a particularly delightful graveyard in its island setting, but very little is known about its history.
6km north-west of Downpatrick.

Moyry Castle, Co. Armagh

The 'Gap of the North' or Moyry Pass was one of the most important ancient routeways into Ulster from the south. Moyry Castle, 3 storeys high, is set on a hilltop overlooking the Gap. The castle was built in 1601 to secure the pass during the Lord Deputy Mountjoy's northern campaign against O'Neill and his followers. It is a small, square tower with rounded corners set in the corner of a partly preserved bawn. The tower is entered by a door on the north-east protected by a gunloop and a machicolation. There are no stairs, reflecting its hurried construction.
12km south-south-west of Newry in Carrickbroad townland.

Audley's Castle, Co. Down

Tower houses are small fortified castles and this one is an impressive defensive structure, standing high on a rocky knoll overlooking the waterway from the Irish sea to Strangford Lough.
Little is known about the castle's early history (it is possibly 15th century in date) but its name comes from its 16th-century owners, the Audley family, who held lands in the area since the 13th century, yet it is unclear if it was they who built the castle.
It was sold to the Ward family in 1646 along with the surrounding estate. By the 19th century the castle was vacant.
12km north-east of Downpatrick off the Strangford Road.

Bonamargy Friary, Co. Antrim

The Franciscan friary ruins stand in a large graveyard with headstones which include memorials to sailors drowned off the coast in the two World Wars. This view shows the east gable of the Friary church, with the remains of an altered east window of just after 1500. To the right is the two-storey east range of the cloister with vaults below and a dormitory above. To the left is the burial vault of the MacDonnell family with a chapel above, added in the 17th century

0.8km east of Ballycastle, surrounded by a golf course.

Monea Castle, Co. Fermanagh

This Scottish-style castle, the finest of the Plantation period in Fermanagh, was built for Malcolm Hamilton in 1618-19, with the bawn added in 1622. It was taken by the Irish in 1641, but was repaired and in 1688 it was the residence of the Governor of Enniskillen. It was abandoned after a fire in the mid-18th century. The castle at the south-east corner of the walled bawn survives almost to its full height. The entrance has two circular towers capped with square chambers. On the ground floor were vaulted rooms and a kitchen with a hall above.

8km north-west of Enniskillen off the road to Belleek.

Old Castle Archdale, Co. Fermanagh

The ruins of a T-shaped house and bawn built by the English planter John Archdale in 1615. It was captured by the Irish in 1641 and finally burned and abandoned in 1689. By 1883 the castle was much as it is now, just a few standing fragments. The heavily restored remains of the house stand at the north end of the bawn. Parts of the east gable and the south wall survive, but the main block is the north stair tower, three storeys high on the south, part of the bawn wall with its wall-walk frame and a semicircular-headed gateway. On the outside is a Latin inscription commemorating the construction by John Archdale.
The site is in Castle Archdale Forest Park off the main Enniskillen-Kesh road, east of Lough Erne.

Old Crom Castle, Co. Fermanagh

The castle had is origins shortly after 1610 when the land was granted to Michael Balfour. In 1619 Captain Pynnar described the castle as a bawn '60 foot square, 12 feet high with two flankers ...there is a house of lime and stone'. In 1689 Crom Castle was besieged twice, but it remained in occupation until finally destroyed by fire in 1764. Only the two northern gables and north-east tower of the 17th-century castle still stand among romantic ruins contrived as early 19th-century garden features.
On a peninsula 5.5 km west-south-west of Newtownbutler.

Tully Castle, Co. Fermanagh

This strong house with wide views over Lough Erne was built between 1610 and 1619 for Sir John Hume. The castle was attacked and burned in 1641 by Rory Maguire and it was never restored. The house survives almost to its full height of two storeys with attics. It is surrounded by a walled bawn some 30m square with four rectangular angle-towers. Much original paving survives within the bawn, which is now laid out in gardens.
Tully is reached off the main Enniskillen to Belleek Road, 4.8km north of Derrygonnelly.

Ballykelly Old Church, Co. Londonderry

This view shows the standing west gable with its small window from outside the graveyard wall. This church was built by the Fishmongers Company of London to serve as the parish church for Tamlaght Finlagan parish (the old church in Mulkeeragh townland was in ruins by 1622). A map of 1622 shows this church, with nave and chancel, but the chancel was replaced in 1719. The church stands beside the Fishmonger's secure house and enclosure, Walworth Bawn, and it was called the Garrison Church, dedicated to St. Peter. It had a stormy history, destroyed in 1641, restored in 1664, destroyed again in 1689 and restored 1689. It was replaced in the 1780s by a fine Gothic church in Ballykelly. The ruin has a good semicircular chancel arch, and a feature of the surrounding graveyard is the many architectural fragments reused as simple gravestones. 0.8 km north-west of Ballykelly at Walworth.

Bellaghy Bawn, Co. Londonderry

Bellaghy Bawn and village were built by Baptist Jones on behalf of the Vintners Company in the years following 1618. This was part of the Plantation by which the Crown encouraged London Guilds to invest in settlements, each of which had to be provided with a fortified enclosure, or 'bawn'. Bellaghy Bawn was a fine example, shown in a map of 1622 with two houses and two big round-corner towers. The area was described in glowing terms with woodlands and waters teeming with fish. Significant remains of the original Bawn survive, including parts of the surrounding wall and one of the large corner towers. The dominating feature in the Bawn today is a large 18th-century house with later additions and a range of outbuildings. These buildings are of such interest that they constitute an integral part of the historic monument and are now used as a visitor centre.
On Deerpark Road, Bellaghy.

Ballycopeland Windmill, Co. Down

This tower mill is an example of a type of industrial building once numerous in the Ards peninsula. It was built towards the end of the 18th century and was worked by the McGilton family. Corn was last ground here in 1915 and the mill was restored to full working order by the Department of the Environment in 1978. It is a provender mill, used mainly to grind animal feed. The cap to which the sails are attached swivelled (in response to the turning of the fantail) on the tower so that the sails kept facing into the wind. Hoppers in the top floor fed grain into three pairs of millstones on the floors below. Beside the mill is the kiln house which has also been restored and is now used as a visitor centre.
1.5km west of Millisle.